A BALANCED MATHEMATICS PROGRAM INTEGRATING SCIENCE AND LANGUAGE ARTS

Unit Resource Guide
Unit 12
Cubes and Volume

THIRD EDITION

KENDALL/HUNT PUBLISHING COMPANY
4050 Westmark Drive   Dubuque, Iowa 52002

A TIMS® Curriculum
University of Illinois at Chicago

UIC The University of Illinois
at Chicago

The original edition was based on work supported by the National Science Foundation under grant No. MDR 9050226 and the University of Illinois at Chicago. Any opinions, findings, and conclusions or recommendations expressed in this publication are those of the author(s) and do not necessarily reflect the views of the granting agencies.

Printed in the United States of America

1 2 3 4 5 6 7 8 9 10   11 10 09 08 07

Letter Home

Cubes and Volume

Date: _____

Dear Family Member:

What kind of structures has your child made with building blocks? houses? towers? skyscrapers? This unit *Cubes and Volume* extends students' experiences with building blocks and poses additional challenges. While constructing models made of cubes, students will make building floor plans and explore the concept of volume. They will use counting strategies for finding the volume of cube structures. As we explore spatial relationships and ways to communicate them, you can provide additional support at home by:

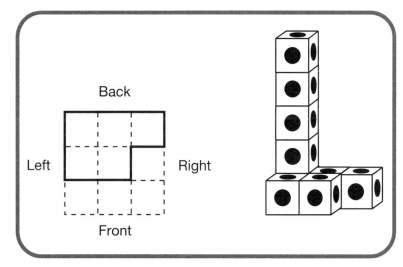

A floor plan for a cube model

- **Comparing Objects.** Find objects around your home for your child to compare. Ask your child which object is taller, which is longer from left to right and front to back, and which has more volume.

- **Copycat Buildings.** You and your child can take turns creating an original building from blocks or sugar cubes and then copying each other's structure. After completing each pair of buildings—the original and the copy—discuss with your child why the structures exactly match or do not match.

Thank you for helping develop your child's mathematical skills.

Sincerely,

_____

Carta al hogar

Cubos y volumen

Fecha: _____

Estimado miembro de familia:

¿Qué clase de estructuras ha construido su hijo/a con cubos? ¿Casas? ¿Torres? ¿Rascacielos? Esta unidad, *Cubos y volumen,* amplía la experiencia de los estudiantes con cubos y presenta nuevos desafíos. Mientras construyen modelos con cubos, los estudiantes harán planos de planta de edificios y explorarán el concepto de volumen. Usarán estrategias de contar para hallar el volumen de estructuras hechas con cubos. Mientras exploramos las relaciones espaciales y las maneras de comunicarlas, usted puede dar su apoyo adicional en casa por medio de las siguientes actividades:

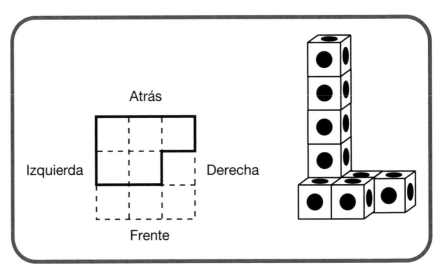

Un plano de planta para un modelo hecho con cubos

- **Comparar objetos.**
  Encuentre objetos en su casa para que su hijo/a los pueda comparar. Pregúntele cuál objeto es más alto, cuál es más largo de izquierda a derecha y del frente hacia atrás, y cuál tiene mayor volumen.

- **Copias de edificios.** Usted y su hijo/a pueden turnarse para crear un edificio original con cubos o con terrones de azúcar y luego copiar la estructura que hizo el otro. Una vez completado cada par de edificios —el original y la copia— hable con su hijo/a acerca de porqué las estructuras coinciden exactamente o no.

Gracias por ayudar a desarrollar las habilidades matemáticas de su hijo/a.

Atentamente,

_____

Table of Contents

Unit 12
Cubes and Volume

Unit 12

Outline
Cubes and Volume

Unit Summary

Estimated Class Sessions **6-7**

Students investigate the variety of buildings they can construct from a fixed volume of eight cubes. They make a data table showing the number of floors in their buildings to help plan a model city. They further explore the concept of volume by building models of classroom objects. The Adventure Book *A World of Cubic Animals* is included in this unit. The DPP includes items that provide practice and assess math facts strategies, especially counting on.

Major Concept Focus

- spatial visualization
- building models
- using models to approximate volume
- communicating solution strategies
- volume in cubic units
- *Adventure Book:* volume in cubic units
- investigating the relationship between volume and shape
- sorting and classifying cube models

Pacing Suggestions

Take advantage of *Math Trailblazers*® connections to other subject areas:

Lesson 4 *A World of Cubic Animals* is an Adventure Book story that reinforces concepts in the unit. Read and discuss the story during language arts.

Assessment Indicators

Use the following Assessment Indicators and the *Observational Assessment Record* that follows the Background section in this unit to assess students on key ideas.

A1. Can students measure volume by counting cubic units?

A2. Can students sort and classify cube models using volume, area of the base, and height?

A3. Do students recognize that different shapes can have the same volume?

A4. Can students construct a cube model from a drawing?

A5. Do students report volumes using numbers and units?

A6. Do students use math facts strategies to add (direct modeling, counting strategies, or reasoning from known facts)?

Unit Planner

	Lesson Information	**Supplies**	**Copies/ Transparencies**

Lesson 1

Skylines

URG Pages 18–29
SG Page 246
DPP A–D

Estimated Class Sessions
2

Activity
Students construct and describe an eight-cube building using different variables: area, volume, and height. They then guide the teacher in making a group data table to display information about a skyline.

Math Facts Strategies
DPP items C and D provide math facts practice.

Homework
Students compare a building they create with ten cubes to one a family member creates.

Assessment
1. Use students' journal entries as an assessment.
2. Use Assessment Indicators A1, A2, and A3 and the *Observational Assessment Record* to document students' abilities to measure volume in cubic units, to sort and classify cube models, and to recognize that different shapes can have the same volume.

Supplies:
• 1 plain cube, such as a block or a sugar cube per student, optional
• 15 same-color connecting cubes per student
• 8 large sheets of paper (11 by 18-inch construction paper or newsprint)
• 1 small cardboard box
• photograph of city skyline, optional

Copies/Transparencies:
• 1 copy of *Two-column Data Table* URG Page 28 per student
• 1 transparency of *My 8-Cube Building* SG Page 246
• 1 copy of *Observational Assessment Record* URG Pages 9–10 to be used throughout this unit

Lesson 2

Cubic Classroom

URG Pages 30–35
SG Pages 247–249
DPP E–F

Estimated Class Sessions
1-2

Activity
Students create cube models of classroom objects to estimate their volumes.

Math Facts Strategies
DPP items E and F provide addition math facts practice.

Homework
Ask students to bring in objects from home to model with connecting cubes. Send home the *Find and Model Objects* Homework Page.

Assessment
Students match cube models and objects. Then they tell which object has the greater volume. Students write their answers in their journals.

Supplies:
• 30 connecting cubes per student
• 1 classroom object per student pair and some for the teacher

Lesson 3

TIMS Towers

URG Pages 36–44
SG Pages 251–257
DPP G–J

Estimated Class Sessions
2

Activity
Students explore strategies for finding the volume of buildings depicted in three-dimensional drawings.

Math Facts Strategies
DPP items H and J assess and provide practice with addition math facts strategies.

Homework
Assign the *Two Towers* Homework Page.

Assessment
1. Students complete the *TIMS Radio Tower* Assessment Page.
2. Use Assessment Indicators A1, A4, and A5 and the *Observational Assessment Record* to document students' abilities to measure volume by counting cubic units, to construct a cube model from a drawing, and to report volumes using numbers and units.

Supplies:
• 200 connecting cubes per student group
• 1 calculator per student

Copies/Transparencies:
• 1 copy of *Individual Assessment Record Sheet* TIG Assessment section per student, previously copied for use throughout the year

	Lesson Information	Supplies	Copies/ Transparencies
	3. Use DPP items H and J to assess the addition math facts in Group B. Use Assessment Indicator A6 and the *Observational Assessment Record* to document students' progress with these facts. 4. Transfer appropriate documentation from the Unit 12 *Observational Assessment Record* to students' *Individual Assessment Record Sheets*.		
Lesson 4 **A World of Cubic Animals** URG Pages 45–51 SG Pages 259–261 AB Pages 57–68 DPP K–L *Estimated Class Sessions* **1**	**Adventure Book** Students find the volume of imaginary animals made of cubes using an interactive book about a young boy's dream. **Math Facts Strategies** DPP item K uses the ten frame for visualization of addition and subtraction facts for 10. **Assessment** Use the *Comparing Ruffy and the Snake* Assessment Page to assess students' thinking about the variables involved in solving the problems. For example, the volume is not necessarily greater if the object is taller or longer.	• 100 connecting cubes per student pair	• 1 transparency of *Ruffy and the Snake* SG Page 259

Preparing for Upcoming Lessons

Weather 2: Winter Skies: continue gathering data about the weather.

Connections

A current list of literature and software connections is available at *www.mathtrailblazers.com*. You can also find information on connections in the *Teacher Implementation Guide* Literature List and Software List sections.

Literature Connections

Suggested Titles

- Murphy, Stuart J. *A House for Birdie.* Harper Collins, New York, 2004.

Software Connections

- *Math Concepts One . . . Two . . . Three!* provides practice with sorting two- and three-dimensional shapes, line symmetry, and finding the missing symmetrical half.
- *Mighty Math Carnival Countdown* provides practice with identifying three-dimensional objects from various perspectives.

Teaching All Math Trailblazers Students

Math Trailblazers lessons are designed for students with a wide range of abilities. The lessons are flexible and do not require significant adaptation for diverse learning styles or academic levels. However, when needed, lessons can be tailored to allow students to engage their abilities to the greatest extent possible while building knowledge and skills.

To assist you in meeting the needs of all students in your classroom, this section contains information about some of the features in the curriculum that allow all students access to mathematics. For additional information, see the Teaching the *Math Trailblazers* Student: Meeting Individual Needs section in the *Teacher Implementation Guide*.

Differentiation Opportunities in this Unit

Journal Prompts

Journal prompts provide opportunities for students to explain and reflect on mathematical problems. They can help both students who need practice explaining their ideas and students who benefit from answering higher order questions. Students with various learning styles can express themselves using pictures, words, and sentences. Teachers can alter journal prompts to suit students' ability levels. The following lessons contain a journal prompt:

- Lesson 1 *Skylines*
- Lesson 3 *TIMS Tower*
- Lesson 4 *A World of Cubic Animals*

Extensions

Use extensions to enrich lessons. Many extensions provide opportunities to further involve or challenge students of all abilities. Take a moment to review the extensions prior to beginning this unit. Some extensions may require additional preparation and planning. The following lessons contain extensions:

- Lesson 2 *Cubic Classroom*
- Lesson 4 *A World of Cubic Animals*

Unit 12

Background
Cubes and Volume

"With well-designed activities, appropriate tools, and teachers' support, students can make and explore conjectures about geometry and can learn to reason carefully about geometric ideas from the earliest years of schooling. Geometry is more than definitions; it is about describing relationships and reasoning. The notion of building understanding in geometry across the grades, from informal to more formal thinking, is consistent with the thinking of theorists and researchers . . . ."

From the National Council of Teachers of Mathematics, *Principles and Standards for School Mathematics*, 2000.

This unit's activities focus on developing spatial visualization, communication skills, and strategies for finding volume. Students find volume by counting the number of cubes that compose an object. They discover that different shapes can have the same volume. Concrete explorations with volume lay the foundation for later study. See the TIMS Tutor: *The Concept of Volume* in the *Teacher Implementation Guide* for further information.

In the first lesson, students discover that a specific volume (8 cubic units) can result in a variety of shapes. Students use connecting cubes to make buildings that have a volume of 8 cubic units. Students also copy their classmates' cube model buildings. They record the area covered by the base of the buildings and then organize the buildings by height, which is measured by the number of floors in each model. Students guide the teacher in making a group data table to display the information.

In the second lesson, students build cube models of classroom objects. They evaluate how closely each cube model reflects the size of the actual object. Students make decisions about whether the model is smaller than, larger than, or very close to the size of the real object.

In the third lesson, students work collaboratively to construct buildings based on three-dimensional drawings. They determine the volume of these buildings using counting strategies, such as grouping the cubes and skip counting.

The concluding lesson features the Adventure Book *A World of Cubic Animals.* In this story Manuel dreams that the animals in his life have changed into animals made of cubes. Students use the drawings in the book to re-create the cubic animals.

Resource

• *Principles and Standards for School Mathematics,* National Council of Teachers of Mathematics. Reston, VA, 2000.

Observational Assessment Record

A1 Can students measure volume by counting cubic units?

A2 Can students sort and classify cube models using volume, area of the base, and height?

A3 Do students recognize that different shapes can have the same volume?

A4 Can students construct a cube model from a drawing?

A5 Do students report volumes using numbers and units?

A6 Do students use math facts strategies to add (direct modeling, counting strategies, or reasoning from known facts)?

A7 _____

Name	A1	A2	A3	A4	A5	A6	A7	Comments
1.								
2.								
3.								
4.								
5.								
6.								
7.								
8.								
9.								
10.								
11.								
12.								
13.								

Name	A1	A2	A3	A4	A5	A6	A7	Comments
14.								
15.								
16.								
17.								
18.								
19.								
20.								
21.								
22.								
23.								
24.								
25.								
26.								
27.								
28.								
29.								
30.								
31.								
32.								

Unit 12

Daily Practice and Problems
Cubes and Volume

A DPP Menu for Unit 12

Two Daily Practice and Problems (DPP) items are included for each class session listed in the Unit Outline. A scope and sequence chart for the DPP is in the *Teacher Implementation Guide*.

Icons in the Teacher Notes column designate the subject matter of each DPP item. Each item falls into one or more of the categories listed below. A menu of the DPP items for Unit 12 follows.

N Number Sense A, B, G, K	✖ Computation G, L	⧗ Time	⬡ Geometry I
⁷₊₃ Math Facts Strategies C–F, H, J, K	$ Money E	✏ Measurement I	◹ Data L

Math Facts Practice and Assessment

In this unit, students practice the addition facts for Group B (3 + 0, 4 + 0, 5 + 0, 4 + 1, 5 + 1, 6 + 1, 5 + 2, 6 + 2, 5 + 3). Facts in Group B can be solved by counting on. See DPP items C, D, E, F, H, and J for practice with these facts. Items H and J can also assess students' fluency with the facts in Group B. Use Assessment Indicator A6 and the *Observational Assessment Record* to document students' progress with these facts.

For more information about the distribution and assessment of math facts, see the DPP Guide in Unit 11 and the TIMS Tutor: *Math Facts* in the *Teacher Implementation Guide.*

Daily Practice and Problems

Students may solve the items individually, in groups, or as a class. The items may also be assigned for homework. The DPPs are also available on the Teacher Resource CD.

Student Questions	Teacher Notes

A **Even or Odd?**

1. Is 6 even or odd? How do you know?

2. Is 13 even or odd? How do you know?

3. Is 17 even or odd? How do you know?

4. Is 26 even or odd? How do you know?

N

Students may use connecting cubes to put together groups of two cubes. If one cube is left over, the number is odd. Encourage students to share their strategies.

1. even
2. odd
3. odd
4. even

B **Fourteen**

Find as many different numbers as possible to complete the statement correctly.

14 is _____ more than _____.

N

14 is 4 more than 10;
14 is 7 more than 7;

Encourage students to use their *100 Charts*. Ask students to share their strategies. Change the starting number. Choose a number less than 20.

Add 0, Add 1

1. A. $3 + 0 = \boxed{}$ B. $4 = 4 + \boxed{}$

   C. $\boxed{} = 5 + 0$ D. $4 + 1 = \boxed{}$

   E. $\boxed{} = 5 + 1$ F. $\boxed{} = 6 + 1$

2. Describe the strategies you use.

1. A. 3   B. 0
   C. 5   D. 5
   E. 6   F. 7

2. Focus discussion on adding zero and adding one.

 Sharing Marbles

1. $5 + 3 = \boxed{}$ 2. $3 + 5 = \boxed{}$

3. $5 - 3 = \boxed{}$ 4. $5 - 2 = \boxed{}$

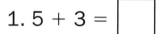

Discuss your strategies.

1. 8   2. 8
3. 2   4. 3

One possible strategy: Using related addition facts to subtract.

Pennies and Dimes

1. 5¢ + 2¢ =

2. 50¢ + 20¢ =

3. 3 + 5 =

4. 30 + 50 =

5. 6¢ + 2¢ =

6. 60¢ + 20¢ =

Students generalized addition and subtraction facts for ten to multiples of ten in Unit 11. Remind students of their work with pennies and dimes in Unit 11 Lesson 2. For example,

5 + 2 = 7 could stand for
2 pennies plus 5 pennies.
50 + 20 = 70 could stand for
2 dimes plus 5 dimes.

1. 7¢	2. 70¢
3. 8	4. 80
5. 8¢	6. 80¢

F **Add 2, Add 3**

1. A. 5 + 2 = ☐   B. ☐ = 6 + 2

    C. 5 + 3 = ☐   D. ☐ = 2 + 5

    E. 3 + 5 = ☐

2. Describe the strategies you use.

1. A. 7   B. 8
   C. 8   D. 7
   E. 8

2. Focus discussion on adding two and adding three.

Sharing Pencils

Mando's mom gave him and his sister a box of 12 pencils for school. If they share the pencils fairly, how many will each get?

6 pencils

 You Can Add

1. A. $6 + 1 = \boxed{}$ B. $5 = 5 + \boxed{}$

   C. $4 + 1 = \boxed{}$ D. $3 + 0 = \boxed{}$

2. Describe your strategy for 1D.

1. A. 7   B. 0
   C. 5   D. 3

2. Answers will vary. Students may say that they know adding zero gives the same number.

 More Volume

Joey made a building from connecting cubes. Its volume was 6 cubic units. Its height was 3 units. Build a building that follows this description. Is there more than one answer?

There is more than one possible answer. Here are two:

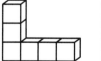

Pass out 6 connecting cubes per student pair. Have students share their solutions.

Student Questions	**Teacher Notes**

 You Can Add Again

1. A. $\boxed{} = 5 + 1$ B. $4 = 4 + \boxed{}$

   C. $5 + 2 = \boxed{}$ D. $5 + 3 = \boxed{}$

   E. $6 + 2 = \boxed{}$

2. Describe your strategy for 1E.

1. A. 6   B. 0
   C. 7   D. 8
   E. 8

2. Answers will vary. One possible response: Counting on by two.

 What's Missing?

1. $\boxed{} + 4 = 10$

2. $2 + \boxed{} = 10$

3. $10 - \boxed{} = 9$

4. $10 - \boxed{} = 3$

Have a transparency of a ten frame and 10 counters available. Invite students to share their strategies and solutions.

1. 6
2. 8
3. 1
4. 7

Student Questions	Teacher Notes

L Weather Data

Use the data in the graph to answer the questions.

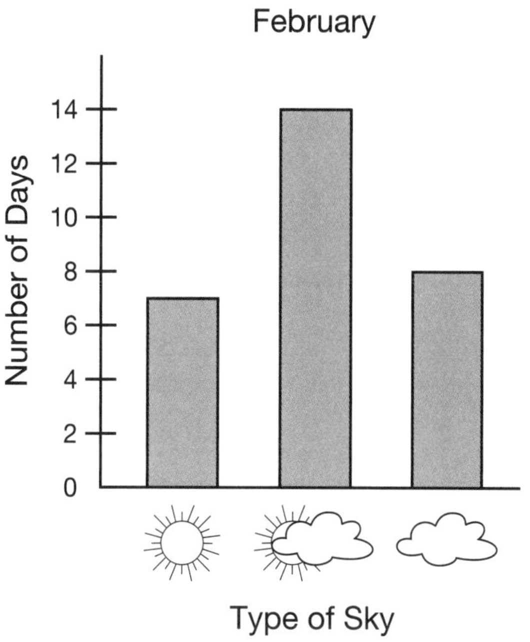
February
Number of Days
0
2
4
6
8
10
12
14
Type of Sky

1. How many days were sunny?

2. What was the weather like most often?

3. How many days were in the month?

Teacher Notes

Students will answer similar questions with their own weather data after your class finishes the data collection for *Weather 2: Winter Skies* which was introduced in Unit 11 Lesson 6.

1. **7 days**
2. **partly sunny**
3. **29 days (add the heights of each bar, 7 + 14 + 8 = 29)**

Skylines

Lesson Overview

Estimated Class Sessions

2

Students form teams to role-play either builders or apprentices. They use connecting cubes to construct buildings that have a volume of 8 cubic units. Team members examine the area of the floor plans of their buildings and organize them by height to create a model skyline. They then construct a group data table to display the information.

Key Content

- Measuring volume by counting cubic units.
- Recognizing that different shapes can have the same volume.
- Sorting and classifying shapes by height.
- Collecting and organizing data in a table.
- Connecting mathematics and real-world situations: creating a model skyline.
- Developing visualization and spatial reasoning skills.

Key Vocabulary

- area
- cube
- cubic units
- face
- floor plan
- height
- square units
- volume

Math Facts Strategies

DPP items C and D provide math facts practice.

Homework

Students compare a building they create with ten cubes to one a family member creates.

Assessment

1. Use students' journal entries as an assessment.
2. Use Assessment Indicators A1, A2, and A3 and the *Observational Assessment Record* to document students' abilities to measure volume in cubic units, to sort and classify cube models, and to recognize that different shapes can have the same volume.

Materials List

Supplies and Copies

Student	Teacher
Supplies for Each Student	**Supplies**
• plain cube, such as a cube-shaped block or a sugar cube, optional • 15 connecting cubes of the same color	• small cardboard box for cube models • photograph of a city skyline, optional • 8 large sheets of paper, e.g., 11 by 18-inch piece of construction paper or newsprint
Copies	**Copies/Transparencies**
• 1 copy of *Two-column Data Table* per student (*Unit Resource Guide* Page 28)	• 1 transparency of *My 8-Cube Building* (*Student Guide* Page 246) • 1 copy of *Observational Assessment Record* to be used throughout this unit (*Unit Resource Guide* Pages 9–10)

All blackline masters including assessment, transparency, and DPP masters are also on the Teacher Resource CD.

Student Books
My 8-Cube Building (*Student Guide* Page 246)

Daily Practice and Problems
DPP items A–D (*Unit Resource Guide* Pages 12–13)

Assessment Tools
Observational Assessment Record (*Unit Resource Guide* Pages 9–10)

Daily Practice and Problems

Suggestions for using the DPPs are on page 25.

A. Even or Odd? (URG p. 12)

1. Is 6 even or odd? How do you know?
2. Is 13 even or odd? How do you know?
3. Is 17 even or odd? How do you know?
4. Is 26 even or odd? How do you know?

B. Fourteen (URG p. 12)

Find as many different numbers as possible to complete the statement correctly.

14 is ___ more than ___.

C. Add 0, Add 1 (URG p. 13)

1. A. $3 + 0 = \boxed{}$
   B. $4 = 4 + \boxed{}$
   C. $\boxed{} = 5 + 0$
   D. $4 + 1 = \boxed{}$
   E. $\boxed{} = 5 + 1$
   F. $\boxed{} = 6 + 1$

2. Describe the strategies you use.

D. Sharing Marbles (URG p. 13)

1. $5 + 3 = \boxed{}$
2. $3 + 5 = \boxed{}$
3. $5 - 3 = \boxed{}$
4. $5 - 2 = \boxed{}$

Discuss your strategies.

1. If you have plain cubes, such as sugar cubes or cube-shaped blocks, distribute these to students instead of connecting cubes for the discussion in Part 1. If you do not have plain cubes, make a large paper cube, and use it as the model.

2. Use connecting cubes to build two shapes with the dimensions shown in Figure 1.

3. Label eight large sheets of paper as shown in Figure 2.

4. Prepare sets of ten connecting cubes in sealable bags for homework.

Part 1 Introduction to Volume

Give each child a single cube or display your large paper cube model. Ask children to describe the cube. To help them analyze the characteristics of a cube, pose the following questions:

- *How many **faces**, or sides, does the cube have?*
- *What is the shape of each face?*
- *How are the faces similar to one another?*

Guide students to describe these attributes: A **cube** has six sides. All the faces are equal length and they have the same size or area.

Once students recognize the basic features of a cube, shift the focus to developing the concept of **volume** as the amount of space that something occupies. Show a single cube and the two shapes you constructed from connecting cubes before the activity, along with a small box. Ask:

- *Would each of these shapes take up the same amount of space in the box?* (No.)
- *What unit would you use to measure the amount of space these different shapes take up in the box?* (cubic unit)
- *How would you measure the amount of space occupied by each shape?* (count the number of cubic units)
- *What is the volume of each of the shapes?* (1 cubic unit, 8 cubic units, 9 cubic units)

Tell students that we measure volume in **cubic units.** For these shapes, one connecting cube is one cubic unit.

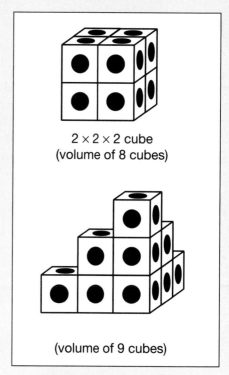

2 × 2 × 2 cube
(volume of 8 cubes)

(volume of 9 cubes)

Figure 1: *Two cube models*

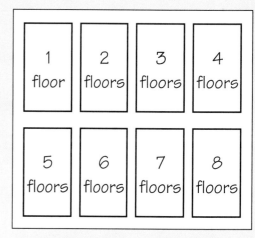

Figure 2: *Paper labeled with the number of floors 1 to 8*

Using 15 cubes of the same color will help students focus on the number of cubes, number of floors, and the shape of the building they are copying. If a student uses different colors to construct a building, his or her apprentice may try to replicate the exact placement of particular colored cubes.

Journal Prompt

What did you learn about cubes and volume?

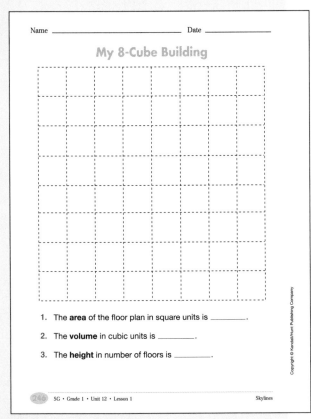

Name _____ Date _____

My 8-Cube Building

1. The **area** of the floor plan in square units is _____.

2. The **volume** in cubic units is _____.

3. The **height** in number of floors is _____.

SG • Grade 1 • Unit 12 • Lesson 1   Skylines

Student Guide - page 246 *(Answers on p. 29)*

Part 2 **Copycat: Builder and Apprentice**

This activity builds spatial visualization and communication skills. Assign students to groups of two or three. Have each team member collect 15 connecting cubes of the same color. Each team member should select a color different from those used by other team members. Tell students that one team member will play the role of the builder and that the other team members will play the roles of apprentices who copy the builder's structure. The builder can use any number of the 15 cubes to construct a building. As the apprentices copy the builder's structure, the builder should observe the progress of the copying procedure and provide appropriate hints to help the other children make an accurate copy. While observing students at work, explain that they can measure the volume of their buildings by counting the number of cubes. Ask each group to report the volume of the building their builder constructed.

Part 3 **Cube Models with a Volume of Eight Cubic Units**

Ask each student to construct a building with eight connecting cubes. Then have students observe their buildings from different vantage points: front, side, back, and top. Ask:

* *Does your building look the same from each point of view?*

Invite student volunteers to describe their buildings to the rest of the class. Encourage other students to add details to the descriptions.

Next, have children place their buildings on the *My 8-Cube Building* Activity Page, lining up the bottom floor of their building with the grid lines. Ask them to look at the buildings from an overhead perspective. Tell them to trace the outline, or the floor plan, of the building and shade the area inside the lines. (See Figure 3.)

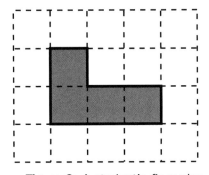

Figure 3: *A student's floor plan*

Some students may recognize that the shaded squares on the grid paper represent the area of the building's floor plan. Emphasize that area is expressed in square units, and have students record the floor plan area of their buildings on the Activity Page. Ask children to raise their hands if their building covers an area of 1 square unit, 2 square units, 3 square units, and so on. Ideally, there will be a variety of areas. Remind students of the units they used to measure area in Unit 10—pennies and square-inch tiles.

Ask about the volume of the buildings. If no child mentions that they are all the same, point out that since every student used eight connecting cubes, the volume of every building is the same—8 cubic units.

Use the variable of height as a way to organize students' buildings. In this activity, height is expressed as the number of floors in the building. Point out that they can describe height using floors as a unit because the cubes are equal in size.

To reinforce the concept of height, have students sit in a large ring. In the center of the ring, place eight large sheets of paper labeled with the number of floors 1 to 8. As you announce each number of floors, ask children to place their buildings on the paper that describes the height of their building. Then, pose the following questions:

- *On which sheet do you see the greatest number of buildings?*
- *Are there buildings that are alike?*
- *How many buildings are alike?*

Encourage students to share their observations with the class as they compare and contrast the buildings displayed in the center of the ring. Students should establish the criteria for deciding what to consider alike and what to consider different. Develop the idea that shape is independent of volume as shown by the variety of shapes made with a volume of eight cubes. Guide the discussion to help children generalize that any given volume (larger than two cubic units) can have a variety of shapes. Remind students of their work in Unit 10 Lesson 2 *Goldilocks and the Three Rectangles* and Lesson 5 *Unit Designs*. Students created designs with 12 square inches and found that a variety of shapes can have the same area.

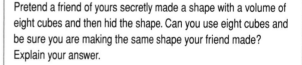

Part 4 Building the Skyline

Tell students that a skyline is the outline of buildings as seen against the sky. If possible, show a photograph of a skyline of Chicago, New York, or another major city. Then, tell students the following story:

Town planners are planning a new town called TIMS Town. They want to have an interesting skyline, using your eight-cube buildings as models. The town planners need your help. They need to know how many buildings of each height were made. A data table can give the planners that information.

The purpose of this part of the activity is to provide a context for children to think through the construction of a data table to display this information. Your role is to guide children as they direct you in constructing the data table on the board.

Remember *not* to draw the data table ahead of time. Ask students the following questions, and use their answers to construct the data table. You may wish to record the students' responses on the board.

- *What are we studying? What information do we have?* (We sorted buildings according to the number of floors. We have information about the number of floors. We know how many buildings have a certain number of floors.)
- *What should the data table look like?* (It should have two columns.)
- *What heading should we use for the first column?* (Number of Floors)
- *What do we know is possible about the number of floors?* (1, 2, 3, 4, 5, 6, 7, or 8 floors)
- *How many rows do we need?* (8 plus 1 for the column headings)
- *What heading should we use for the second column?* (Number of Buildings)
- *What information, or data, should we put in the second column? What did we find out as we put our shapes on the large sheets of labeled paper?* (the number of buildings for each number of floors)
- *What should we name the data table?* (TIMS Town Skyline)

Have children use the *Two-column Data Table* to record the information.

Conclude the activity by discussing other ways students could have classified their buildings. You may wish to offer the following suggestions:

There are many interesting ways to describe and organize the buildings you made. We could have sorted the buildings by the area of the floor plan, length, or width instead of height (the number of floors tall). We picked height because we were interested in making a skyline.

Math Facts Strategies

DPP items C and D practice addition math facts. Item D relates addition and subtraction sentences.

Homework and Practice

• Have students use ten cubes to make a building in class. They can keep their buildings in their school desks. Give each student a set of ten cubes in a sealable bag for their families to make a building. When students return to school, they will compare the 10-cube buildings they made in class to the 10-cube buildings their family members made as homework.

• DPP item A reviews even and odd numbers. Item B encourages students to use "more than" to compare numbers.

Assessment

• Use students' journal entries to assess students' understanding of the idea that different shapes can have the same volume.

• Place several cube models in a learning center in your classroom. Have students record the height and volume of each model on an index card.

• Use the *Observational Assessment Record* to document students' abilities to measure volume by counting cubic units; sort and classify cube models using volume, area of the floor plan, and number of floors; and recognize that different shapes can have the same volume.

TIMS Town Skyline

Number of Floors	Number of Buildings
1	
2	
3	
4	
5	
6	
7	
8	

Figure 4: *TIMS Town Skyline data table*

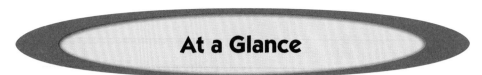

At a Glance

Math Facts Strategies and Daily Practice and Problems

DPP items A and B build number sense. Items C and D practice math facts.

Part 1. Introduction to Volume

1. Ask children to describe a cube.
2. Tell students that **volume** is the amount of space that something occupies.
3. Show a connecting cube, a larger cube made of nine connecting cubes, a third shape constructed from connecting cubes, and a small box. Discuss which shape would take up more space in the box.

Part 2. Copycat: Builder and Apprentice (A1)

1. Assign students to groups of two or three.
2. One team member, as the builder, uses at most 15 cubes to construct a building.
3. The apprentice copies the builder's structure while the builder observes and provides appropriate hints to help the other child make an accurate copy.
4. Students measure the volume of their buildings by counting the number of cubes.
5. Each group reports the volume of their buildings.

Part 3. Cube Models with a Volume of Eight Cubic Units (A2) (A3)

1. Each student constructs a building with eight connecting cubes and describes it.
2. Students place their buildings on the *My 8-Cube Building* Activity Page, trace the outline (the floor plan) of the building on the grid, and shade the area inside the lines.
3. Students report the area of the floor plans in square units to the class. The volume of every building is the same—eight cubic units.
4. Students organize their buildings by height.
5. Students compare and contrast the buildings displayed. Through discussion children generalize that any given volume can have a variety of shapes.

Part 4. Building the Skyline (A3)

1. Tell students that town planners will use their buildings to create a new TIMS Town.
2. Guide students as they direct you in constructing a data table with information about their buildings. Discuss other ways students can classify their buildings.

At a Glance

Homework

Students compare a building they create with ten cubes to one a family member creates.

Assessment

1. Use students' journal entries as an assessment.
2. Use Assessment Indicators A1, A2, and A3 and the *Observational Assessment Record* to document students' abilities to measure volume in cubic units, to sort and classify cube models, and to recognize that different shapes can have the same volume.

Answer Key is on page 29.

Notes:

Name _____ Date _____

_____

Two-column Data Table, Blackline Master

Student Guide (p. 246)

My 8-Cube Building

Answer will vary.*

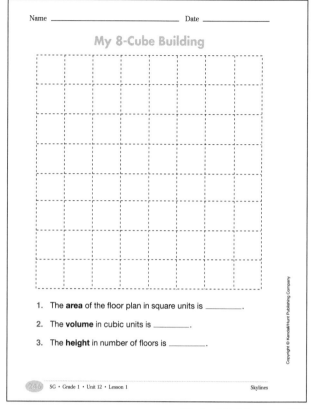

Student Guide - page 246

---

*Answers and/or discussion are included in the Lesson Guide.

Lesson 2

Cubic Classroom

Student pairs use connecting cubes to build models of classroom objects. Students then estimate the volume of these objects by finding the number of cubes in their models. They then decide if the volume of their models is the same as, less than, or greater than that of the classroom objects.

Key Content

- Measuring volume in cubic units.
- Estimating volume by building cube models for objects.
- Connecting mathematics to real-world situations: building models of classroom objects.
- Comparing volumes.
- Developing visualization and spatial reasoning skills.
- Using geometric modeling to solve problems.
- Communicating mathematics orally and in writing.

Key Vocabulary

- approximate
- model

Math Facts Strategies

DPP items E and F provide addition math facts practice.

Homework

Ask students to bring in objects from home to model with connecting cubes. Send home the *Find and Model Objects* Homework Page.

Assessment

Students match cube models and objects. Then they tell which object has the greater volume. Students write their answers in their journals.

Materials List

Supplies and Copies

Student	Teacher
Supplies for Each Student • 30 connecting cubes **Supplies for Each Student Pair** • classroom object	**Supplies** • classroom objects
Copies	**Copies/Transparencies**

All blackline masters including assessment, transparency, and DPP masters are also on the Teacher Resource CD.

Student Books

Cube Models (*Student Guide* Page 247)
Find and Model Objects (*Student Guide* Page 249)

Daily Practice and Problems

DPP items E–F (*Unit Resource Guide* Page 14)

Daily Practice and Problems

Suggestions for using the DPPs are on page 33.

E. Pennies and Dimes (URG p. 14)

1. 5¢ + 2¢ =
2. 50¢ + 20¢ =
3. 3 + 5 =
4. 30 + 50 =
5. 6¢ + 2¢ =
6. 60¢ + 20¢ =

F. Add 2, Add 3 (URG p. 14)

1. A. 5 + 2 = ☐
   B. ☐ = 6 + 2
   C. 5 + 3 = ☐
   D. ☐ = 2 + 5
   E. 3 + 5 = ☐

2. Describe the strategies you use.

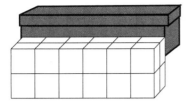

Chalkboard or Whiteboard Eraser

volume of cube model = 24 unit cubes

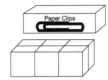

Paper Clip Box

volume of cube model = 6 unit cubes

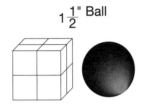

$1\frac{1}{2}$" Ball

volume of cube model = 8 unit cubes

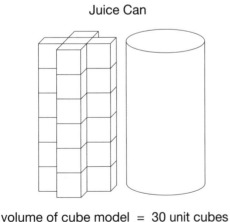

Juice Can

volume of cube model = 30 unit cubes

Figure 5: *Examples of classroom objects*

Before the Activity

Collect classroom objects that are no bigger in volume than 30 connecting cubes. The objects should also have a reasonably simple shape. You will need to have at least one object for each pair of students. Rectangular objects will be easier to model than uneven ones. See Figure 5 for examples.

Teaching the Activity

Display the classroom objects for students to observe. Discuss which objects can be modeled reasonably accurately with cubes (like an eraser or box) and which can only be approximated. Tell each student pair to select one object. Have students draw a picture of the object on the *Cube Models* Activity Page. Next, have pairs use connecting cubes to build a life-size model of the object. Each partner should make a model of the same object.

To estimate the volume of the object, students can count the cubes of the model. Then, by deciding whether their model is *the same as, less than,* or *greater than* the size of the classroom object, they can **approximate,** or estimate, its volume. Have students record the information on the *Cube Models* Activity Page.

Name _____ Date _____

Cube Models

1. Select an object. Then, draw a picture of it.

2. Make a **life-size** cube model of the object.

3. Count the cubes to find the volume of the model. The

   volume of my cube model is _____.

4. Is the volume of the cube model **the same as**, **less than**, or **greater than** the volume of the real object? The **volume** of

   my cube model is _____ that of
   the real object.

Cubic Classroom   SG • Grade 1 • Unit 12 • Lesson 2   247

Student Guide - **page 247** *(Answers on p. 35)*

Math Facts Strategies

DPP items E and F provide addition math facts practice. Item F also uses money and multiples of ten.

Homework and Practice

Encourage students to bring in an object that they can model with connecting cubes. Tell students that the objects should not be larger than those they modeled in class. The *Find and Model Objects* Homework Page provides a description of the activity.

Assessment

Show two objects and their cube models. Encourage students to match the appropriate object to its model. Then, challenge students to tell which object has the greater volume. Students may write their answers in their journals.

Extension

Have students arrange all their models on a table. Students can then guess the object that each model was based on and estimate the volume. They can also rank the objects according to volume

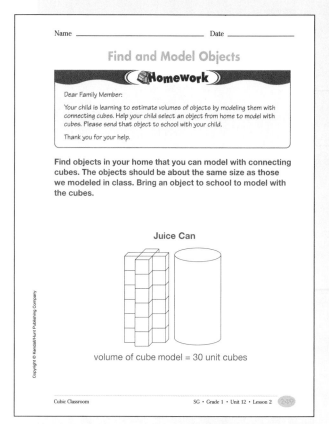

Student Guide - page 249

Estimated Class Sessions 1-2

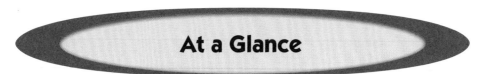 **At a Glance**

Math Facts Strategies and Daily Practice and Problems

DPP items E and F provide addition math facts practice.

Teaching the Activity

1. Students select an object to model with connecting cubes.
2. Students model objects with connecting cubes and estimate their volume.
3. Students tell if the model's volume is equal to, less than, or greater than the object's volume.
4. Students draw a picture of their object and record information about the object and its cube model on the *Cube Models* Activity Page.

Homework

Ask students to bring in objects from home to model with connecting cubes. Send home the *Find and Model Objects* Homework Page.

Assessment

Students match cube models and objects. Then they tell which object has the greater volume. Students write their answers in their journals.

Extension

Have students guess what object each model was based on and estimate the volume of each model.

Answer Key is on page 35.

Notes:

Student Guide (p. 247)

Cube Models

Answers will vary.*

Name _____ Date _____

Cube Models

1. Select an object. Then, draw a picture of it.

2. Make a **life-size** cube model of the object.

3. Count the cubes to find the volume of the model. The
   volume of my cube model is _____.

4. Is the volume of the cube model **the same as**, **less than**, or
   greater than the volume of the real object? The **volume** of
   my cube model is _____ that of
   the real object.

Cubic Classroom   SG • Grade 1 • Unit 12 • Lesson 2   247

Student Guide - page 247

*Answers and/or discussion are included in the Lesson Guide.

Lesson 3

TIMS Towers

Lesson Overview

Students work in teams to build cube models based on three-dimensional drawings. Students explore various counting strategies for finding the volume of their cube models.

Key Content

- Measuring volume in cubic units.
- Reporting volumes using numbers and units.
- Translating between different representations of shapes (three-dimensional drawings and cube models).
- Grouping and counting objects.
- Using geometric modeling to solve problems.
- Developing visualization and spatial reasoning skills.
- Communicating mathematics orally and in writing.

Key Vocabulary

- three-dimensional drawing

Math Facts Strategies

DPP items H and J assess and provide practice with addition math facts strategies.

Homework

Assign the *Two Towers* Homework Page.

Assessment

1. Students complete the *TIMS Radio Tower* Assessment Page.
2. Use Assessment Indicators A1, A4, and A5 and the *Observational Assessment Record* to document students' abilities to measure volume by counting cubic units, to construct a cube model from a drawing, and to report volumes using numbers and units.
3. Use DPP items H and J to assess the addition math facts in Group B. Use Assessment Indicator A6 and the *Observational Assessment Record* to document students' progress with these facts.
4. Transfer appropriate documentation from the Unit 12 *Observational Assessment Record* to students' *Individual Assessment Record Sheets*.

Materials List

Supplies and Copies

Student	Teacher
Supplies for Each Student • calculator **Supplies for Each Student Group** • 200 connecting cubes	**Supplies**
Copies	**Copies/Transparencies**

All blackline masters including assessment, transparency, and DPP masters are also on the Teacher Resource CD.

Student Books
TIMS Towers 1 (*Student Guide* Page 251)
TIMS Towers 2 (*Student Guide* Page 252)
TIMS Towers Data Table (*Student Guide* Page 253)
Two Towers (*Student Guide* Page 255)
TIMS Radio Tower (*Student Guide* Page 257)

Daily Practice and Problems
DPP items G–J (*Unit Resource Guide* Pages 15–16)

Assessment Tools
Observational Assessment Record (*Unit Resource Guide* Pages 9–10)
Individual Assessment Record Sheet (*Teacher Implementation Guide*, Assessment section)

Daily Practice and Problems

Suggestions for using the DPPs are on pages 40–41.

G. Sharing Pencils (URG p. 15)

Mando's mom gave him and his sister a box of 12 pencils for school. If they share the pencils fairly, how many will each get?

H. You Can Add (URG p. 15)

1. A. 6 + 1 = ☐

   B. 5 = 5 + ☐

   C. 4 + 1 = ☐

   D. 3 + 0 = ☐

2. Describe your strategy for 1D.

I. More Volume (URG p. 15)

Joey made a building from connecting cubes. Its volume was 6 cubic units. Its height was 3 units. Build a building that follows this description. Is there more than one answer?

J. You Can Add Again (URG p. 16)

1. A. ☐ = 5 + 1

   B. 4 = 4 + ☐

   C. 5 + 2 = ☐

   D. 5 + 3 = ☐

   E. 6 + 2 = ☐

2. Describe your strategy for 1E.

Have students work in teams of two to four members. Have students preview the three-dimensional drawings of the four buildings on the *TIMS Towers 1* and *2* Activity Pages. Encourage students to think of various strategies they can use for finding the volumes of these buildings. Point out that counting by ones is not the easiest way to find the answer.

Tell teams to make a model of Tall Tower and to record the volume on the *TIMS Towers Data Table* Activity Page. Then, invite students to share their solution paths with their classmates. Some possible strategies follow:

- Grouping by columns (counting by tens: 10, 20, add 2 = 22)

- Grouping by rows (counting by twos: 2, 4, 6, 8, 10, 12, 14, 16, 18, 20, 22)

- Using the constant feature (repeating equal key) on the calculator ($\boxed{2}$ $\boxed{+}$ $\boxed{2}$ $\boxed{=}$ $\boxed{=}$ …)

As students discuss their strategies and report the volume of the tower, encourage them to use a number and a unit (cubes).

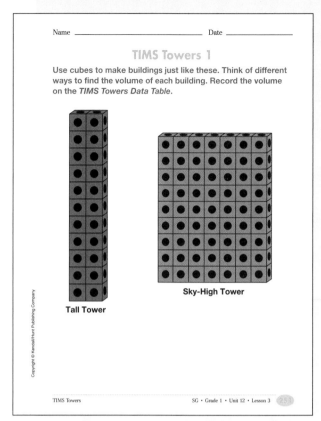

Student Guide - page 251

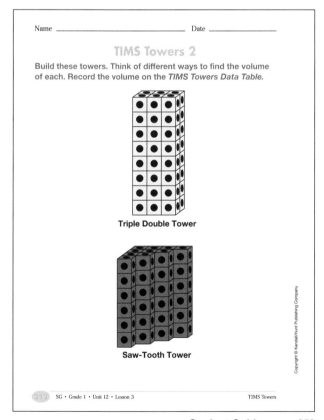

Student Guide - page 252

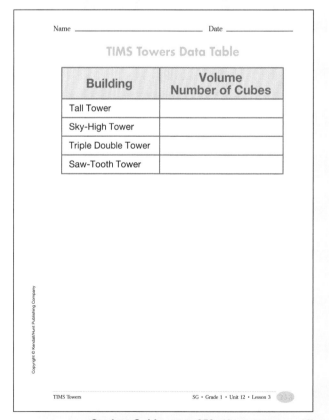

Building	Volume Number of Cubes
Tall Tower	
Sky-High Tower	
Triple Double Tower	
Saw-Tooth Tower	

Student Guide - page 253 *(Answers on p. 43)*

Repeat this procedure for Sky-High Tower, Triple Double Tower, and Saw-Tooth Tower. As students work through each problem, foster their originality. Ask, *"Is there another way to find the volume?"* Conclude the activity by inviting the class to analyze the similarities and differences among the different problem-solving strategies presented.

Math Facts Strategies

DPP items H and J assess students' use of addition math facts strategies.

Homework and Practice

*   Assign the *Two Towers* Homework Page. Students must find the volume of two models and tell which model has the greater volume and height. Remind students to report the volumes using a number and a unit (cubes).

*   DPP item G explores division in a word problem about sharing. Item I explores the concept that different shapes can have the same volume.

Name _____ Date _____

Two Towers

(Homework)

Find the volume of each tower.

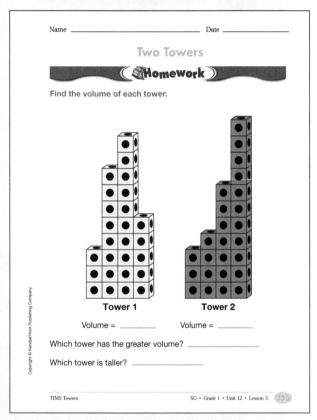

Tower 1   Tower 2

Volume = _____   Volume = _____

Which tower has the greater volume? _____

Which tower is taller? _____

TIMS Towers   SG • Grade 1 • Unit 12 • Lesson 3   255

Student Guide - page 255 *(Answers on p. 43)*

- The *TIMS Radio Tower* Assessment Page can be used as one measure of students' abilities to find the volume and height of an object in a three-dimensional drawing and to communicate their solution paths.

- Use the *Observational Assessment Record* to document students' abilities to measure volume by counting cubic units and to construct a cube model from a drawing.

- Use DPP items H and J to assess students' use of strategies with the addition math facts in Group B. Counting on is an appropriate strategy for these facts. Document students' progress on the *Observational Assessment Record*. Note which strategies students use.

- Transfer appropriate documentation from the Unit 12 *Observational Assessment Record* to students' *Individual Assessment Record Sheets*.

Name _____ Date _____

TIMS Radio Tower

TIMS Radio Tower

Height = _____

Volume = _____

How did you find your answer?

_____

_____

_____

_____

TIMS Towers   SG • Grade 1 • Unit 12 • Lesson 3   257

Student Guide - page 257 *(Answers on p. 44)*

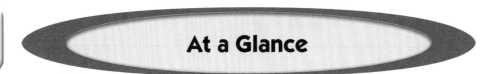

Estimated Class Sessions **2**

At a Glance

Math Facts Strategies and Daily Practice and Problems (A6)

DPP items H and J assess and practice addition math facts strategies. Item G explores division. Item I explores volume measurement.

Teaching the Activity (A1) (A4) (A5)

1. Students discuss strategies for finding the volume of the models on the *TIMS Towers 1* and *2* Activity Pages.
2. Student teams use connecting cubes to make models of the towers and find their volumes.
3. Students record the volumes on the *TIMS Towers Data Table* Activity Page.
4. Students analyze the different problem-solving methods.

Homework

Assign the *Two Towers* Homework Page.

Assessment

1. Students complete the *TIMS Radio Tower* Assessment Page.
2. Use Assessment Indicators A1, A4, and A5 and the *Observational Assessment Record* to document students' abilities to measure volume by counting cubic units, to construct a cube model from a drawing, and to report volumes using numbers and units.
3. Use DPP items H and J to assess the addition math facts in Group B. Use the Assessment Indicator A6 and the *Observational Assessment Record* to document students' progress with these facts.
4. Transfer appropriate documentation from the Unit 12 *Observational Assessment Record* to students' *Individual Assessment Record Sheets*.

Answer Key is on pages 43–44.

Notes:

Student Guide (p. 253)

TIMS Towers Data Table

Building	Number of Cubes
Tall Tower	22
Sky-High Tower	63
Triple Double Tower	48
Saw-Tooth Tower	60

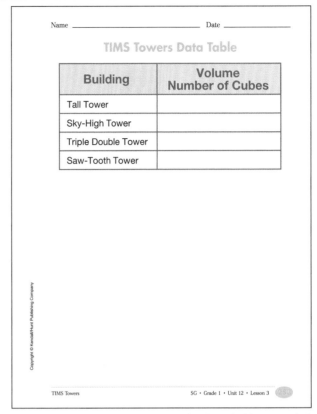

Name _____ Date _____

TIMS Towers Data Table

Building	Volume Number of Cubes
Tall Tower	
Sky-High Tower	
Triple Double Tower	
Saw-Tooth Tower	

TIMS Towers   SG • Grade 1 • Unit 12 • Lesson 3

Student Guide - page 253

Student Guide (p. 255)

Two Towers

The volume of Tower 1 is 26 cubes. The volume of Tower 2 is 25 cubes. Tower 1 has the greater volume. Tower 2 is the tallest.

Name _____ Date _____

Two Towers

Homework

Find the volume of each tower.

Tower 1   Tower 2

Volume = _____   Volume = _____

Which tower has the greater volume? _____

Which tower is taller? _____

TIMS Towers   SG • Grade 1 • Unit 12 • Lesson 3

Student Guide - page 255

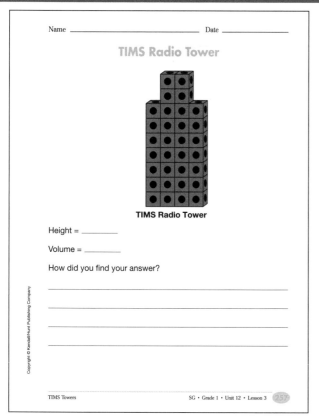

Name _____ Date _____

TIMS Radio Tower

TIMS Radio Tower

Height = _____

Volume = _____

How did you find your answer?

_____
_____
_____
_____

TIMS Towers   SG • Grade 1 • Unit 12 • Lesson 3   257

Student Guide - page 257

Student Guide (p. 257)

TIMS Radio Tower

Height is 9 cubes. Volume is 32 cubes. Solution strategies will vary.

Lesson 4

A World of Cubic Animals

Lesson Overview

Estimated Class Sessions

1

In this *Adventure Book* story, Manuel tells his family about his experiences using cubes to create different shapes with the same volume. Later that night, he has a strange dream: He imagines that animals have been transformed into creatures made of cubes. Manuel now realizes he can find the volume of these animals simply by counting the cubes. His dream turns into a nightmare when he changes into a cubic person and cannot return to his human form. After his mother awakens him, he is happy to discover that he is still Manuel, a human boy.

Key Content

- Measuring and reporting volume in cubic units.
- Translating between different representations of shapes (three-dimensional drawings and cube models).
- Grouping and counting objects.
- Using geometric modeling to solve problems.
- Developing visualization and spatial reasoning skills.
- Communicating mathematics orally and in writing.
- Connecting mathematics and language arts: reading a story about measuring volume.

Math Facts Strategies

DPP item K uses the ten frame for visualization of addition and subtraction facts for 10.

Assessment

Use the *Comparing Ruffy and the Snake* Assessment Page to assess students' thinking about the variables involved in solving the problems. For example, the volume is not necessarily greater if the object is taller or longer.

Materials List

Supplies and Copies

Student	Teacher
Supplies for Each Student Pair • 100 connecting cubes	**Supplies**
Copies	**Copies/Transparencies** • 1 transparency of *Ruffy and the Snake* (*Student Guide* Page 259)

All blackline masters including assessment, transparency, and DPP masters are also on the Teacher Resource CD.

Student Books

Ruffy and the Snake (*Student Guide* Page 259)
Comparing Ruffy and the Snake (*Student Guide* Page 261)
A World of Cubic Animals (*Adventure Book* Pages 57–68)

Daily Practice and Problems

DPP items K–L (*Unit Resource Guide* Pages 16–17)

Daily Practice and Problems

Suggestions for using the DPPs are on page 49.

K. What's Missing? (URG p. 16)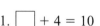

1. $\boxed{} + 4 = 10$

2. $2 + \boxed{} = 10$

3. $10 - \boxed{} = 9$

4. $10 - \boxed{} = 3$

L. Weather Data (URG p. 17)

Use the data in the graph to answer the questions.

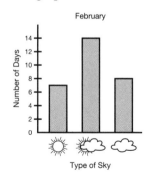

1. How many days were sunny?
2. What was the weather like most often?
3. How many days were in the month?

Page 58

- *How does Manuel know that the two different shapes he made have the same volume?*

Adventure Book - page 58

Page 61

- *What is the volume of each of the horse's legs?*

Each leg has a volume of 10 cubes. (Include the hooves.)

- *Which is an easier way to find the volume of the horse's legs, counting by ones or counting by twos?*

Adventure Book - page 61

Adventure Book - page 63

Adventure Book - page 68

Page 63

- *What is the volume of the giraffe's neck?*

The volume of the giraffe's neck is 12 cubes.

Page 68

- *Why does Manuel say it is easy to find the volume of things made of cubes?*

Answers will vary.

- *What is the volume of Ruffy's dog bone?*

The volume of the dog bone is 9 cubes.

Journal Prompt

Write a story in which you dream about animals made of cubes. Tell how you count the cubes to find their volume.

Math Facts Strategies

DPP item K uses the ten frame for visualization of addition and subtraction facts for 10.

Homework and Practice

DPP item L practices interpreting a bar graph and addition computation.

Assessment

Have students turn to the *Comparing Ruffy and the Snake* Assessment Page in their *Student Guides.* Display a transparency of the *Ruffy and the Snake* Activity Page on the overhead projector, and have students closely study the illustrations of the animals. Then, turn off the projector and read aloud the first question on the Assessment Page. Remind students to refer to the drawings of Ruffy and the snake on the *Ruffy and the Snake* Activity Page. Each student should independently describe the comparison between Ruffy and the snake. Have children write their responses before they work on the second question. Next, ask students to work in pairs to build and find the volume of Ruffy and the volume of the snake.

The main purpose of this assessment is to understand students' thinking. Students' answers provide you with a basis to assess their reasoning process. Their responses should reflect their abilities to think about the variables that are involved in solving the problems. For example, volume is not necessarily greater because an object is longer or taller.

TIMS Tip

If children compare the animals' volumes to one another, you can discuss this observation by posing the following questions: *Do these animals compare in volume to one another in the same way as animals you would see in real life? Do you think that Manuel would have approximately the same volume as a giraffe? Does a horse have about the same volume as an elephant?* Emphasize that because Manuel is dreaming, things appear different than they do in real life.

Student Guide - page 259

Student Guide - page 261 (Answers on p. 51)

- Student pairs can build and find the volume of the cubic characters illustrated in the *Adventure Book* and record the information on a class data table as shown in Figure 7.

VOLUME OF CUBIC CHARACTERS

Animal	Volume
Ruffy the dog	23 cubes
Bell the horse	134 cubes
wolf	37 cubes
snake	23 cubes
giraffe	96 cubes
elephant	145 cubes
Manuel	89 cubes

Figure 7: *Class Data Table for* A World of Cubic Animals

- Six animals and Manuel are represented as cube models in the *Adventure Book*. Student pairs can make cube models of other kinds of animals. They can display their models labeled with the name of the animal and the number of cubes used.

Student Guide (p. 261)

Comparing Ruffy and the Snake*

1. Answers will vary.

2. Ruffy's volume is 23 cubes. The snake's volume is also 23 cubes.

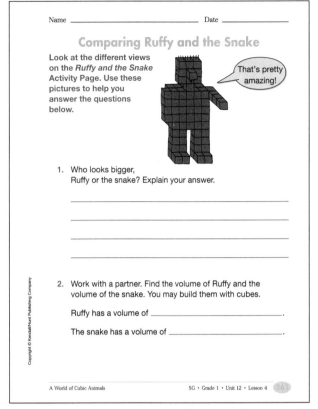

Student Guide - page 261

*Answers and/or discussion are included in the Lesson Guide.

Glossary

This glossary provides definitions of key vocabulary terms in the Grade 1 lessons. Locations of key vocabulary terms in the curriculum are included with each definition. Components Key: URG = *Unit Resource Guide* and SG = *Student Guide*.

A

Approximate (URG Unit 12)
1. (adjective) a number that is close to the desired number
2. (verb) to estimate

Area (URG Unit 10; SG Unit 12)
The amount of space that a shape covers. Area is measured in square units.

B

C

Capacity (URG Unit 9)
1. The volume of the inside of a container.
2. The largest volume a container can hold.

Circle (URG Unit 2)
A curve that is made up of all the points that are the same distance from one point, the center.

Circumference (URG Unit 15)
The distance around a circle.

Coordinates (URG Unit 19)
(In the plane) Two numbers that specify the location of a point on a flat surface relative to a reference point called the origin. The two numbers are the distances from the point to two perpendicular lines called axes.

Counting All (URG Unit 1)
A strategy for adding in which students start at one and count until the total is reached.

Counting Back (URG Unit 8)
A method of subtraction that involves counting from the larger number to the smaller one. For example, to find 8 − 5 the student counts 7, 6, 5 which is 3 less.

Counting On (URG Unit 1 & Unit 4)
A strategy for adding two numbers in which students start with one of the numbers and then count until the total is reached. For example, to count 6 + 3, begin with 6 and count three more, 7, 8, 9.

Counting Up (URG Unit 8)
A method of subtraction that involves counting from the smaller number to the larger one. For example, to find 8 − 5 the student counts 6, 7, 8 which is 3 more.

Cube (URG Unit 12 & Unit 15)
A solid with six congruent square faces.

Cubic Units (URG Unit 12)
A unit for measuring volume— a cube that measures one unit along each edge. For example, cubic centimeters and cubic inches.

cubic centimeter

Cylinder (URG Unit 15)
A three-dimensional figure with two parallel congruent circles as bases (top and bottom) and a curved side that is the union of parallel lines connecting corresponding points on the circles.

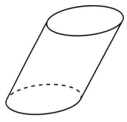

D

Data Table (URG Unit 3)
A tool for recording and organizing data on paper or on a computer.

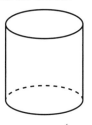

Name	Age

Division by Measuring Out (URG Unit 14)
A type of division problem in which the number in each group is known and the unknown is the number of groups. For example, twenty students are divided into teams of four students each. How many teams are there? (20 students ÷ 4 students per team = 5 teams) This type of division is also known as measurement division.

Division by Sharing (URG Unit 14)
A type of division problem in which the number of groups is known and the unknown is the number in each group. For example, twenty students are divided into five teams. How many students are on each team? (20 students ÷ 5 teams = 4 students per team) This type of division is also known as partitive division.

E

Edge (URG Unit 15)
A line segment where two faces of a three-dimensional figure meet.

Equivalent Fractions (URG Unit 18)
Two fractions are equivalent if they represent the same part of the whole. For example, if a class has 8 boys and 8 girls, we can say $\frac{8}{16}$ of the students are girls or $\frac{1}{2}$ of the students are girls.

Even Number (URG Unit 4 & Unit 13)
Numbers that are doubles. The numbers 0, 2, 4, 6, 8, 10, etc. are even. The number 28 is even because it is 14 + 14.

F

Face (URG Unit 12 & Unit 15)
A flat side of a three-dimensional figure.

Fixed Variables (URG Unit 2, Unit 6 & Unit 11)
Variables in an experiment that are held constant or not changed. These variables are often called controlled variables.

G

H

Hexagon (URG Unit 2)
A six-sided polygon.

I

J

K

L

Length (URG Unit 6 & Unit 10)
1. The distance along a line or curve from one point to another. Distance can be measured with a ruler or tape measure.
2. The distance from one "end" to another of a two- or three-dimensional figure. For example, the length of a rectangle usually refers to the length of the longer side.

Line
A set of points that form a straight path extending infinitely in two directions.

Line Symmetry (URG Unit 7 & Unit 18)
A figure has line symmetry if it can be folded along a line so that the two halves match exactly.

Line of Symmetry (URG Unit 7 & Unit 18)
A line such that if a figure is folded along the line, then one half of the figure matches the other.

M

Making a Ten (URG Unit 13)
A strategy for adding and subtracting that takes advantage of students' knowledge of partitions of ten. For example, a student might find 8 + 4 by breaking the 4 into 2 + 2 and then using a knowledge of sums that add to ten.

$$8 + 4 =$$
$$8 + 2 + 2 =$$
$$10 + 2 = 12$$

Median (URG Unit 6 & Unit 9)
The number "in the middle" of a set of data. If there is an odd number of data, it is the number in the middle when the numbers are arranged in order. So the median of {1, 2, 14, 15, 28, 29, 30} is 15. If there is an even number of data, it is the number halfway between the two middle numbers. The median of {1, 2, 14, 15, 28, 29} is $14\frac{1}{2}$.

Mr. Origin (URG Unit 19)
A plastic figure used to help childen learn about direction and distance.

N

Near Double (URG Unit 13)
A derived addition or subtraction fact found by using doubles. For example, 3 + 4 = 7 follows from the fact that 3 + 3 = 6.

Number Sentence (URG Unit 3 & Unit 4)
A number sentence uses numbers and symbols instead of words to describe a problem. For example, a number sentence for the problem "5 birds landed on a branch. Two more birds also landed on the branch. How many birds are on the branch?" is 5 + 2 = 7.

O

Odd Number (URG Unit 4)
A number that is not even. The odd numbers are 1, 3, 5, 7, 9, and so on.

Origin (URG Unit 19)
A reference point for a coordinate system. If the coordinate system is a line, we can determine the location of an object on the line by the number of units it is to the right or the left of the origin.

P

Part (URG Unit 4)
One of the addends in part-part-whole addition problems.

Pattern Unit (URG Unit 7)
The portion of a pattern that is repeated. For example, AAB is the pattern unit in the pattern AABAABAAB.

Perimeter (URG Unit 6; SG Unit 12)
The distance around a two-dimensional shape.

Polygon
A closed, connected plane figure consisting of line segments, with exactly two segments meeting at each end point.

Polygons   Not Polygons

Prediction (URG Unit 5)
Using a sample to predict what is likely to occur in the population.

Prism (URG Unit 15)
A solid that has two congruent and parallel bases. The remaining faces (sides) are parallelograms. A rectangular prism has bases that are rectangles. A box is a common object that is shaped like a rectangular prism.

Q

Quadrilateral
A polygon with four sides.

R

Rectangle (URG Unit 2)
A quadrilateral with four right angles.

Rhombus (URG Unit 2)
A quadrilateral with four sides of equal length.

Rotational Symmetry (URG Unit 7)
A figure has rotational (or turn) symmetry if there is a point on the figure and a rotation of less than 360° about that point so that it "fits" on itself. For example, a square has a turn symmetry of $\frac{1}{4}$ turn (or 90°) about its center.

S

Sample (URG Unit 5)
Some of the items from a whole group.

Sphere (URG Unit 15)
A three-dimensional figure that is made up of points that are the same distance from one point, the center. A basketball is a common object shaped like a sphere.

Square (URG Unit 2)
A polygon with four equal sides and four right angles.

Symmetry (URG Unit 18)
(See Line Symmetry, Line of Symmetry, and Rotational Symmetry.)

T

Three-dimensional Shapes (URG Unit 15)
A figure in space that has length, width, and height.

TIMS Laboratory Method (URG Unit 5)
A method that students use to organize experiments and investigations. It involves four components: draw, collect, graph, and explore. It is a way to help students learn about the scientific method. TIMS is an acronym for Teaching Integrated Mathematics and Science.

Trapezoid (URG Unit 2)
A quadrilateral with exactly one pair of parallel sides.

Trial (URG Unit 6)
One attempt in an experiment.

Triangle (URG Unit 2)
A polygon with three sides.

Turn Symmetry
(See Rotational Symmetry.)

U

Using Doubles (URG Unit 13)
A strategy for adding and subtracting which uses derived facts from known doubles. For example, students use 7 + 7 = 14 to find that 7 + 8 is one more or 15.

Using Ten (URG Unit 13)
A strategy for adding which uses reasoning from known facts. For example, students use 3 + 7 = 10 to find that 4 + 7 is one more or 11.

V

Variable (URG Unit 2 & Unit 11)
A variable is something that varies or changes in an experiment.

Volume (URG Unit 9 & Unit 12; SG Unit 12)
1. The amount of space an object takes up.
2. The amount of space inside a container.

W

Whole (URG Unit 4)
The sum in part-part-whole addition problems.

X

Y

Z